The River

The River

Poems by

Sandra Noel

Kelsay Books

© 2017 Sandra Noel. All rights reserved. This material may not be reproduced in any form, published, reprinted, recorded, performed, broadcast, rewritten or redistributed without the explicit permission of Sandra Noel. All such actions are strictly prohibited by law.

Cover art: "Sunrise on the Rappahannock"
by Summers Bohenstiel © May 18, 2014

ISBN:13- 978-1-947465-13-8

Kelsay Books
Aldrich Press
www.kelsaybooks.com

For Yvonne
the girl who loved horses
September 1950 - November 2013

Acknowledgments

From the Depths, a Story Will Rise: "The River," Haunted Waters Press, NO. 18, 2015
The Gypsy in my Kitchen, chapbook: "River II," and "The Veil," Finishing Line Press, July, 2015

Contents

Night Train	1
The River	2
Thin Ice	4
Fireflies	6
Fox and Hounds	7
Hoar Frost	8
A Spring Evening in Virginia	9
"A leaf, a stone..."	10
The Field	12
The Tilt-A-Whirl	13
How to Explain	14
Before the Deluge	15
Inside the Antique Bookshop	16
A Stitch in Time	17
When No One's Looking	19
The Horses on the Hill	21
I Never Asked the Right Questions	22
Leaving the Mending	23
Watermarked Heart	24
We Have Almost Nothing in Common	25
The Veil	26
The River II	28
Honeysuckle	29
Blackberry Island	30
What Comes After	31

*Once you brought me a river.
It flowed through your hands and into mine
on its way to the sea.*

*Your gifts were always that way,
beautiful and impossible to hold.*

Night Train

Rolling out of Union station
followed by a crescent moon
on the cutting edge of night
steel wheels on steel rails
a hard hold on reality
and homeward bound
watching as darkness fades
into city lights and shadows
on the platforms
celluloid memories
of my childhood flicker by.

The River

A case for saving it from an expat Virginian

Soul deep
the Rappahannock
winding through a lost city.
Even as a child
that river made me weep.
Sometimes a thing so close
can make us feel
without understanding.

The river carried my dreams westward
but much later
for a while it was, how shall I say this
bliss...
slow and lazy in summer.
Firefly fireworks danced over sandy banks
where we'd drink bootlegged sloe gin
the color of blood.

The earth in that land was full of blood
and ghosts rose with the moonlight.
Our pastel summer dresses
bleached white by it
trailed ghostly in the dark water
as we waited for sunrise.
In winter the ice was thick near shore
where we'd skate late into the evening
under a sky full of stars.

My river dreams, I lost them all
dreamed others, held and lost some too.
From the window of this plane

I watch it wind its snake brown body
through the damaged landscape of my childhood.
It wraps around what has come to claim it
as it wrapped around my heart
ever changing, moving seaward.

Thin Ice

A cup of hot chocolate
reminds me of Virginia winters
and the river where we used to skate
arm in arm inside yellow crime tape barriers
between us and thin ice near its center.
Oil barrels filled with scrap wood
burned on shore to warm our frozen fingers.

Nothing freezes for long
in our Northwest winters
and ice covering this small pond
is more hazard than useful
but still I place my weight on the rotted edge
hear the sound crack of danger.

A boy we all knew and admired for his daring
once wandered past the yellow tape.
He must have heard that sound
just before the ice gave way
and the river's seaward current
always grasping, always moving
carried him under and away.

We still went down to the river
winter after winter, the yellow tape
replaced with more impressive barriers
but there were always those
who tested the boundaries
skated past, jumped over, fell in.
The river didn't mind a bit
collecting our dead
giving up even the rescued reluctantly

holding on with icy fingers
while the rest of us, less adventurous
kept where the ice was solid and safe.

*I step back from the edge
watch the crack, swift as lightning
grow under my boot print
and across the pond's dark surface
hear a familiar sound
like small arms fire echo in the distance.*

Fireflies

As girls, we'd run out
into sweltering summer evenings
after dinner
while our mothers
gathered in the day
brought mason jars to capture fireflies
as they emerged one by one
in the dusky darkness
to make lamps of them
or stick them in our hair
and dance the firefly dance
another kind of girls gone wild
until our Mothers called us in.

Sometimes we'd find them
dark and dead on our pillows in the morning–
a transformation as astonishing
as waking up ordinary girls
not goddesses, our hair full of stars.

Fox and Hounds

I have tried on all the faces
of my childhood
the ones that used to fit
none bear up
so left to my own devices
silent, wary
a fox in the shadows
luxurious, motionless
until the sharp reports of Autumn
are silenced by an early snow
covering shattered branches and bones alike
rendering them beautiful.
I make my retreat
on the cold silent earth
away, away into the woods
leaving tracks for anyone to follow.

Hoar Frost

On barn roofs
the bare oak and chestnut trees
fence posts
the crunch under our boots
on the way to the barn.

Everything glittered under a cobalt sky
the horses standing in a circle of steam
from their warm breath
making them more magical in our eyes.

You were not even imagined then
nor all the other losses that would follow
just the sharp chill in the air
and smell of leather soap
the barn freshly cleaned
and the horses, God, the horses!

A Spring Evening in Virginia

Across the field
you could hear them
their weighted foot falls
an occasional spark
of metal shoe on gravel
as they approached the barn
dancing shadows appeared
magical, as always
then the smell and feel of them
that great restrained strength
expectant, leaning into our hands
as we opened the stall doors
and settled them in for the night
rustling the smooth oats and fresh hay.
We were so young then
and took such joy for granted
or maybe we thought
joy was just life, until later
we were taught to
endure
surrender
accept.

"A leaf, a stone..."

After re-reading *Look Homeward Angel*, by Thomas Wolfe.

When I come back
again some day
I will come back
to an empty house
no, someone else's house
once a kind of happy prison
when I was young
more and more
as I grow older
a memory of love, of comfort
why I fled
I cannot say
what fueled that flight
from love
that ended in such darkness
and dragging them, for a while anyway
into it.

It was never my intention
to strike out
anyway, but alone
but we are never alone
if we ever experienced love
broken or otherwise.
Its tendrils in that country
cling like the honeysuckle vines
growing as they are
in that guilty, blood-soaked soil
clinging to stones and walls
and hearts.

My family began
with a great love
that ended in a graveyard
for they were angels before
they passed into angel territory
breaking the ties
however unwillingly
that held us all together.

The Field

There was a field
past the horse barns and houses
surrounded by oak and chestnut trees
long since chopped down
for lesser things.

Ghosts lived in the branches
we could hear them at dusk
and I wonder where they go
to rest where now there is nothing
but noise and dust.

In summer those trees
shaded out the heat and humidity
in the fall, they blazed with golden light
and we would ride all day
and into sundown
listening for the voices in the trees
a chorus of souls rising from the earth
settling in the branches.

The Tilt-A-Whirl

In my small town
a carnival arrived every August
with ramshackle thrill rides and handlers
a little too drunk to run machinery
but we rode anyway
while our parents strode aisles
full of barkers and gritty side shows
buying cotton candy when we returned
breathless.

Not so long after
my whole world tilted sideways
and I had to learn to walk again
on an uneven, shifting surface
falling so often just trying to walk.
Then one day I learned to dance.

How to Explain

Why you quit college
in your senior year
and drank every night
to make the nightmares stop
until it didn't help anymore
not that it ever really did
married the most impossible
of possibilities
just because he'd asked
and you felt no one would again
and divorced because you got better
took self-defense classes
and finally finished college
bought a gun then traded it in
for a pair of good running shoes.
Wait! NO!
If anyone asks just tell them
you got hit by a bus or cancer
not your fault either but this explanation
may be less stressful on the listener.
I mean, who wants to hear about rape?
It's such a "college co-ed cliché"
as someone once responded.

Before the Deluge

She was a soft target
Cinderella of the streets
hair bowed like her lips
a painted heart-shaped face
pale as a Geisha's
in the neon flashing overhead
her uneasy wobble on unsteady feet
towards the waiting car.

For a moment, out of context
she is still somebody's Princess
in her first new pair of slippers
before life swept her off her feet
into a deluge of trouble
tearing her loose
and into the flood.

Inside the Antique Bookshop

Andrew the owner, a Vietnam veteran
sits in an old swivel chair
talking about why he likes Charles Bukowski
and how poetry saved him
forty years ago, from offing himself
how he hates hearing people say
you should just, GET OVER IT!
who never had to and we talk about
how most people who never experience real violence
try to create it with horror movies or thrill rides
and the room feels like a confessional
too close for any kind of comfort
He says he thinks I understand violence
and I do but decide not to make any confessions
as I want no absolution from him or anyone else
so I buy the Bukowski
and read a few lines before starting my car.
Poetry is absolution enough.

A Stitch in Time

My Mother's stitches
so perfect once
when I was seventeen
her hands on the hem
her mouth full of pins
and advice
I wish I had taken.

While other Mothers scoured local shops
with more money than sense
my Mother created
out of bolts of tulle and silk
from old patterns she found
in Vogue and Mademoiselle
snipping and gathering it all together
into something original, magical.

I still remember that dress
(not the boy or the dance)
and wonder what she dreamed for me
before her eyes became too weak
to see through the needle's eye
how she felt when I'd arrive home
after long absences, out west
with my badly patched jeans
and home spun ideas.

After her funeral
going through her life box by box
I found it again folded in tissue
ran my fingers over hundreds
of her tiny perfect stitches.

That dress looks just the same
unlike the original wearer.
Not a wrinkle on its white silk surface.
Not a stitch undone.

When No One's Looking

Sundays, I think of my Mother
once so beautiful
auburn haired and curvy
my Father's dream
until the day he died in her arms.
The cancer would not wait
and she could not follow he said
until it was her time
but he'd be waiting.

Now she sits alone
back cruelly curved by time and arthritis.
By day she does a dozen
ordinary things with dignity
if not the grace she once possessed.
At night she reaches over, holds his hand
when no one's looking
hears the songs he wrote for her
played on his guitar.

In her dreams they are still lovers
driving the coast highway
in their 1937 Chevy
and sometimes feels the fabric
of the wings she sewed
for a wrecked bi-plane
they re-built and flew together
into a hundred sunsets.

She sees the sunset from her chair
in the small living room
where they used to sit together

when the cancer would not wait
and he said she could not follow
until it was her time.
She is not afraid.
She's sure he's waiting
with his old guitar and flying gear
his easy smile.
She smiles back, waves sometimes
when no one's looking.

The Horses on the Hill

You rest in your silver frame
smiling back at me
or really
at the young man
with the camera
who asked you for a photo
before he left for war.

I wanted to say goodbye
but was too late
and so I make these little alters.
There are candles and a Buddha
and images of your happiness
just nothing to hold on to.

Well, for a little while longer, Mother
just a while
the horses on the hill
their heads down in a hard rain
remember?

I Never Asked the Right Questions

As you flew through the hours
days and years of our lives
bright as an angel
until you landed
then your colors faded a little
muted by responsibilities
of family and income.

I did not understand until later
and much later, too late
the answers came
on their own into my life
how to balance love of work
and love of those around us.

I loved flying with you
because I saw your true self
free of the landscape
created by earthly love.
Had I asked, I know your answers
would be part truth and part lies
as mine have always been.

Leaving the Mending

We are polite, if not familiar
I ask to stay in the house
and you stay too
settle your heavy, broken body
into our Mother's chair
waiting me out.
We are strangers, nothing new
we always were.

Memories still attach these walls
line the bottoms of drawers
in the corners, the closets
she is all around us.
I wish we could connect
her love to our sisterly estrangement
but the dance is the dance
and there is no time or willingness
to learn new steps.

We move around each other carefully
pulling at frayed seams and patchwork.
Grief has knitted us together
for this short time
but we both know
once the work is done
nothing will be mended.

Watermarked Heart

You were so solid
I engraved my dreams
on your heart
and they would be there
forever I thought
but the years fell away
like my dreams so quickly
leaves in a dry season
and you began to fade
first pale when the illness struck
then translucent
leaving a watermark
on my heart
forever.

We Have Almost Nothing in Common

She calls about her fibromyalgia
and another boring evening with a fixer-upper
how her dog barks all night
and keeps her awake
and I wonder why we are still friends
remembering high school
and the beautiful girl the other girls hated
because she was not wearing Villager clothes
or carrying a Gucci bag
and going to her house after school
where her father sat in stony silence
when we were introduced
and later, the bruises she showed only me
her beautiful eyes spilling over
streaks through the heavy makeup
she never needed
except to hide them.

We have almost nothing in common
but kept in touch over the years
and recently she arrived just in time to save me
after weeks in my Mother's emptying house
drove up and loaded me into
her shiny new SUV under protest
talked non-stop though dinner
until all I could do was listen and forget
what I was leaving behind, for a while anyway.
She is still beautiful, nothing, not her hard youth
nor death to brain cancer of a husband she adored
has put a mark on her that lasted.

The Veil

I conjured you
from stardust and moonshine
patty-caked and pretty
like Jehovah's own Ken Doll
baptized in the muddy-watered
dreams of my childhood
where voodoo queen grandmothers
drunk on gin and real power
tucked us in at night
with lullabies and bloody-feathered fingers
rattled the bones in our nightmares
but brought us candy when we cried.

I licked you dry,
drop by holy rolly drop
till you stood naked, shivering, almost alive
but just before I kissed your eyelids open
hesitated, hearing rattling on the wind
rough laughter and a warning
so I slid a silken veil
over your well-formed head
and placed you in my heart instead
silent and beautiful these many years
veil intact and shimmering with hope.

Until one night
I found you human-formed
in an earthly kind of hell
where fallen angels danced to the music you played
on the devil's own instrument
drowning out the rattle in my ancestral bones
and longing, like poor Orpheus

one foot out of hell and looking back
I gazed into your unveiled eyes
and could not look away.

The River II

When we arrived it was evening
the air was thick with mayflies
barn swallows dive-bombing overhead
eagles by the hundreds in trees beside the river.
It was a movie set for a love story
ending in tragedy
but at the time it was only evening
and no one knew how it would end
as we walked hip deep
in a field of soft rush
making whisper sounds
as we passed through.
You asked me the names
of insects and stars
as if I had some kind of unique knowledge.
Well, the insects were mine
but not the stars
and you listened like a child
as I told you stories of the river people
the mayflies and their kin
who spend most of their brief lives submerged
then transform into wings for a single flight
into the swarm to mate
fall back into the river and die.
As we walked slowly back
in the chilly air darkness,
I did not know brevity or loss, only hope
as swallows feasted on love spent insects.
Later I was reminded of that day
how some pass unnoticed
while others burn into our memories
with such perfect painful clarity.

Honeysuckle

On my grandmother's farm
the smell and first wild thing
I ever tasted
that did not come from a store
tangled among the blackberries
we collected in five-gallon buckets.
Black snakes thick as my wrists
patrolled the patch
but she frightened them off
with a hickory stick
pushed hard into the sweet vines.

I wonder now, was she brave
or just practical, fit for the times.
To me she was a goddess
with her long grey hair
pinned up and covered until bedtime.
She'd let me brush it out at night
while she told stories
of my mother and her sisters,
my mother always the heroine.
I wonder sometimes
if she would be as proud of me
following a path she could not imagine
from that hard scrabble farm in North Carolina
to this island in an inland sea.

She was so strong, a woman
raising nine kids alone
in the worst of times
and some said she'd grown hard
but I remember her taking me gently
by the hand into the wide fields,
"Here, child, taste...this is sweet!"

Blackberry Island

On one hot afternoon
we swam downstream to meet it
into that heavy current, deceptively slow
what were we thinking
but we were only twenty
we were not thinking much
rolling in the river's ambivalence
reaching the island gasping, laughing
but the way back was no joke
taking all of our young body strength
to reach even the shore nearby
then stumbling back on shaky legs
to where we started
down the old Falmouth Road to our car
still laughing as the young do
after near death experiences.

What Comes After

In an uneasy silence
we stood alone together
waiting for a train.
You had said all you could say
and I said nothing.

No one knew me better
or understood me less.
The mirror image of our lives
had cracked.
The train headed westward
and you drove home alone.

You are gone to earth
but I see you in the sky
wings rocking to a country song
long gone and yet right here.
The distance was in miles
not spirit.

About the Author

Sandra Noel works as an illustrator and graphic designer developing interpretive and wayside exhibits for national parks, forest and other organizations involved in environmental education. Her poetry has appeared in Pontoon, Barnwood International Poetry Magazine, Buddhist Poetry Review, Outside In Literary and Travel Magazine and Elohi Gadugi Journal and others and two chapbooks, "The Gypsy in my kitchen," and "Into the green," published by Finishing Line Press.

www.ingramcontent.com/pod-product-compliance
Lightning Source LLC
LaVergne TN
LVHW021626080426
835510LV00019B/2777